The Secret Life of
CLOUDS
and other wonderful weather forms

happy yak

© 2025 Quarto Publishing Group USA Inc.
Text © 2025 Moira Butterfield
Illustrations © 2025 Vivian Mineker Chen

Moira Butterfield has asserted her right
to be identified as the author of this work.
Vivian Mineker Chen has asserted her right
to be identified as the illustrator of this work.

Senior Designer: Sarah Chapman-Suire
Commissioning Editors: Carly Madden and Emily Pither
Editor: Laura Knowles
Consultant: Ben Ballin
Creative Director: Malena Stojić
Associate Publisher: Rhiannon Findlay
Senior Production Controller: Elizabeth Reardon

First published in 2025 by Happy Yak,
an imprint of The Quarto Group.
100 Cummings Center, Suite 265D.
Beverly, MA 01915, USA.
T (978) 282-9590 F (978) 283-2742
www.quarto.com

EEA Representation, WTS Tax d.o.o.,
Žanova ulica 3, 4000 Kranj, Slovenia.

ISBN 978-1-83600-114-0

Manufactured in Guangdong, China TT042025
9 8 7 6 5 4 3 2 1

FSC
www.fsc.org

MIX
Paper | Supporting
responsible forestry
FSC® C016973

CONTENTS

DEAR READER
5

WHEN I WAS BORN
6

ME AND MY CLOUD FRIENDS
8

THE CLOUD DRAGONS
A weather tale from China
10

UMBRELLA DAYS
12

THE GREAT RAIN JOURNEY
14

I SEE A RAINBOW!
16

THE RAINBOW TREASURE POT
A weather tale from Ireland
18

HOW TO CATCH FOG
20

VISIT A CLOUD FOREST
22

THE KING OF THE CLOUD FOREST
A weather tale from Central America
24

SNOW DAYS
26

BRRR! ICE!
28

SOPHIE AND THE BARBEGAZI
A weather tale from Switzerland
30

WHICH WAY, WIND?
32

WATCH OUT: STORMS ABOUT!
34

WHIRLING WEATHER
36

TIGER, TIGER, THE WIND IS COMING!
An African American weather tale
38

SUNSHINE DAYS
40

LIVING IN A HOT HOME
42

THE CLOUD-SCRAPING LADY
A weather tale from Canada
44

BE A WATER AND CLOUD FRIEND
46

Hello. I'm Casper the cloud.
I'm like a ball of fluff in the sky,
or a squishy pillow that can fly!
Float with me. We'll have some fun,
come wind or rain. Come snow or sun!

Dear reader,

Are you ready for a floaty journey? I'm going to show you what it's like to be a puffy cloud like me, high up in the sky. I want you to see what I see!

On our trip we'll discover some of the secrets of the weather happening all around us every day. We'll be visiting rainy plains, foggy deserts, and cloudy forests—and we'll be meeting fog-drinking beetles, snowmen, and cloud families.

I've heard lots of magical weather stories on my travels and I'll tell you some of them as we go along. There will be tales of cloud dragons, a trickster leprechaun, a skiing gnome, and a greedy tiger!

Are you ready for a cloud ride with me? Let's go!

Casper the cloud

Look for
CASPER'S FLOATING FACT
clouds along the way. They will pop up to tell you extra facts that will amaze you.

WHEN I WAS BORN

My journey around and around

I was born thanks to the Sun.

Clouds appear because the Sun warms the world's water—in its rivers, lakes, and seas.

evaporation

1. The warmth turns the liquid water into a gas called water vapor. This process is called evaporation. The water vapor drifts up into the air, but you can't see it.

2. As the water vapor floats higher and higher into the air, it starts to cool down. As it cools, it turns into tiny droplets.

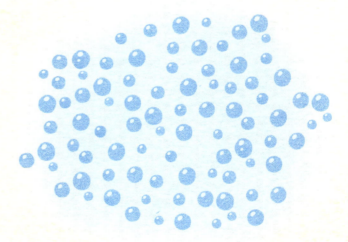

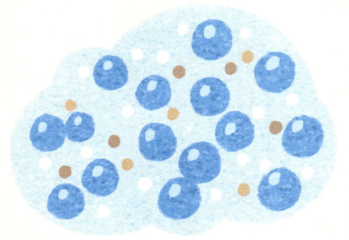

3. The droplets gather around specks of dust and salt floating in the air. They begin to join together and grow bigger, making a cloud—just like me.

Here I am!

But I won't be here for long. Soon I'll change and begin again. Here's how...

My droplets will bump into each other, getting bigger. Eventually, they will become so heavy that they will fall as rain and run into the world's rivers, lakes, and seas.

The Sun will heat up the water and the cloud-making will start all over again. Perhaps I'll be remade as a different-shaped cloud.

There's a name for the way water goes around and around between the sky and Earth. It's called the water cycle. I'm part of it!

around and around

around and around

CASPER'S FLOATING FACT

On average, a water droplet in a cloud is about a quarter as wide as a human hair.

ME AND MY CLOUD FRIENDS
Puffy, feathery, streaky, rainy!

The shape and size of a cloud depend on many things, such as how strong the wind is and how cold the air is. There are lots of different types of clouds, but they all belong in five main cloud families. Here are a few you might spot.

Clouds that billow upward, like me, have names starting with **cumulo** (kyoo-myoo-loh). It means *heaped* in Latin. We are usually found low in the sky.

I am a small **cumulus** cloud with a flattish bottom and a fluffy top. I usually turn up in good weather.

I have a much bigger cousin called a **cumulonimbus** cloud. It piles up high into the sky and has a flat top. It signals stormy weather.

High clouds have names starting with **cirro** (sur-oh). It means *wisp of hair* in Latin.

Cirrus clouds are in this family. They look like feathery streaks high up in the sky. They often signal that the weather is about to change.

Medium-height clouds have names starting with **alto**. That means *high* in Latin.

Altocumulus clouds are small cloudlets that line up in rows. They sometimes signal the weather is changing.

Clouds that look like wide sheets across the sky have names starting with **strato**. It means *layers*.

Stratocumulus clouds fill the sky in a lumpy-looking gray layer. They often bring rain.

Clouds that are going to bring rain or snow often have names starting with **nimbo**. It means *fog* or *cloud*.

Nimbostratus clouds are thick, dark, and filled with raindrops. If you see them, you should find your umbrella!

CASPER'S FLOATING FACT

Altogether, there are more than 100 different types of clouds.

THE CLOUD DRAGONS

A weather tale from China

The day legends came to life

In Chinese legend, magical dragons look after the world's weather and waters. Cloud dragons weave their way across the sky, bringing rain where it's needed. This story is inspired by a traditional cloud dragon tale.

Long ago, Emperor Wu had a new temple built. Around that time, a young man called Zhang arrived at the court. He was a very skilled artist, so Wu asked him to make wall paintings for the new temple.

"I want four cloud dragons, as realistic as if they had just flown down from the sky," commanded Wu.

Zhang painted four cloud dragons—one on every wall inside the temple. They were very fine Chinese dragons, with the body of a snake, horns, a snout, and shining scales. They trailed cloud, just as if they were moving through the heavens.

When Emperor Wu arrived to see the work, he clapped his hands in delight. "Wonderful! Wonderful! All they need is their eyes painted in. When will you finish them?" he asked.
Zhang shook his head. "If I paint in their eyes, they will come to life," he replied. The emperor scoffed. "Don't be silly. They must have eyes," he ordered.

Zhang sighed and did as he was told. He began by painting the eyes on two of the cloud dragons...

CRACK!

Instantly, two of the temple walls split and shattered. The two cloud dragons had come to life! Their scales rippled and their tails swung as they flew toward the door, trailing billows of cloud behind them.

"Stop! I command you to stop!" Wu shouted at them, but they streaked away, turning the sky red and gold as they went.

Zhang stepped forward to paint the eyes on the other dragons, but the emperor rushed to stop him. "No! No! I was wrong," he cried. Zhang nodded. "Cloud can't be controlled or commanded by anyone, and it's the same with cloud dragons," Zhang replied. "It's best just to admire them, especially these ones. Otherwise, your temple is going to fall down!"

UMBRELLA DAYS
Splish, splash! It's raindrop time.

I've gathered some raindrop secrets for you, to make rainy days lots more interesting!

Raindrops aren't really teardrop-shaped. As they fall, air pushes up on them, and they end up flat along the bottom and curved across the top, like the top half of a burger bun.

Raindrops usually don't get much bigger than 0.2 inches (6 mm) wide (about as wide as a small raisin). The fattest raindrops ever measured stretched 0.3 inches (8.6 mm) across, but that's unusual.

Rain is powerful! Over millions of years it can wear down rock, carving it into different shapes.

The rainiest place in the world is Mawsynram in India. There, the average yearly rainfall is 39 feet (11.9 m). That's nearly six times the height of a door in your home!

It might seem strange, but the driest place in the world is chilly Antarctica. There's a rocky area there, called the Dry Valleys, where it hasn't rained for two million years! There's hardly any ice or snow in that part of Antarctica, either.

Without rain, plants and animals couldn't live on Earth. We don't know if rain falls on other planets, but we do know that our planet is very lucky that it has rainy days.

It's possible to make it rain by cloud-seeding. This is when an aircraft drops tiny crystal particles into clouds to help raindrops form.

When rain hits the ground, plant oils are released into the air. They're called petrichor (pet-ruh-core), and they create the fresh, earthy scent you can sometimes smell when it rains after a period of dry weather.

CASPER'S FLOATING FACT

Most clouds don't rain. Their water vapor just drifts away in the sky, perhaps to make new cloud shapes.

THE GREAT RAIN JOURNEY
Following the rain clouds

In some parts of the world, monsoon rain clouds bring heavy rain each year. They trigger one of the most amazing animal journeys on the planet. Let's follow it!

All about monsoons

Monsoon rains are seasonal, which means they happen at certain times every year. Parts of Africa, Asia, Central America, and northern Australia all have monsoons. Each year, the extra-rainy weather brings much-needed water for the plants, animals, and people.

Africa has two huge plains that stretch between Tanzania and Kenya. They are called the Serengeti and the Masai Mara. More than two million animals that live on the plains spend their lives following the seasonal monsoon rains, looking for green grass to eat.

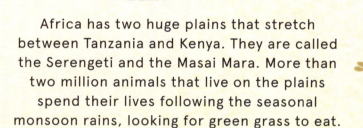

Wildebeest, zebras, and other grazing animals such as gazelles all have their babies in January and February in the southern Serengeti. Around half a million wildebeest babies are born each year.

In March, the monsoon rains end in the southern Serengeti, and the grass begins to dry up. All the animals start a long walk to the Masai Mara, where the rains have begun to fall.

Around October, they will come back to the southern Serengeti. Altogether, they travel 1,200 miles (1,900 km) or more in a giant circle, following the rains. It's called the **Great Migration**.

FOLLOW THE RAIN! FOLLOW THE RAIN!

Around 400,000 zebras also make the Great Migration journey, following the rain clouds.

During February, as many as 8,000 wildebeest calves are born every day on the Serengeti.

Grant's gazelle

Thomson's gazelle

Around 300,000 Grant's and Thomson's gazelles and 12,000 eland antelopes are on the trip, too.

Eland antelope

Hungry hunters such as lions and hyenas follow the journeying animals, trying to grab a meal.

The animals must cross the Mara River on their trip, but over 3,000 hungry crocodiles lie in wait underwater, hoping to grab them!

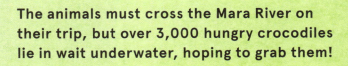

CASPER'S FLOATING FACT

More than 40 percent of the world's people live in places where monsoon rains fall every year.

I SEE A RAINBOW!
Bouncy light and brilliant colors

Rain can be annoying when it stops you from going outside. Remember, though, that there's a wonderful upside to rain. It can give you rainbows!

What makes a rainbow?

You need the Sun behind you and raindrops in front of you for the chance to see a rainbow. As the sunlight shines through the raindrops, it bends, like a ball hitting a wall and bouncing off in a different direction. Though light might seem "white," it is actually made up of seven colors. Each color bends slightly differently. The colors back out of the raindrops side by side in seven curves.

sunlight

white light

raindrop

seven colors

RED

ORANGE

YELLOW

GREEN

BLUE

INDIGO

VIOLET

Next time you see a rainbow, look for all these colors.

There are fewer rainbows in winter, when raindrops are more likely to turn into snowflakes. Light doesn't split into different colors when it reflects through snowflakes.

SOME OTHER SPECIAL BOWS

A rainbow cloud

When light shines through small water droplets or ice crystals in a thin cloud.

A double rainbow

One above and one below. The colors in the top one are reversed.

A moonbow

Created by moonlight, which isn't as strong as sunlight. A moonbow is usually very faintly colored.

A fogbow

These are usually white, as the fog droplets are too tiny to split the light into seven colors.

Earth is the only planet we know of that has rainbows. What a lucky place to live!

Most rainbows don't last long, but one record-breaker lasted nine hours.

CASPER'S FLOATING FACT
Rainbows are thought to be lucky in many parts of the world.

17

THE RAINBOW TREASURE POT

A weather tale from Ireland

Hidden gold and a clever trick

Have you heard that there's a pot of gold hidden at the end of a rainbow? The tale I'm going to tell you will reveal the secret! It's based on an Irish legend of a small magical person called a leprechaun.

Leprechauns love treasure, and they've been hiding it ever since the first king of Ireland dropped a gold coin from his pocket and a leprechaun grabbed it from the grass. If you corner a leprechaun, he might promise you treasure, but beware. Leprechauns are tricksters!

One day, a farmer and his wife caught a leprechaun stealing a bowl of milk in their dairy.
"Grab him!" cried the farmer. "We'll throw him in a sack and take the wriggling thief to jail!"
"I'll grant you a wish if you let me go. Any wish at all," replied the leprechaun.

The farmer and his wife agreed, and they both thought for a while.
"Come on now. I don't have all day. It's starting to rain and I need to get home," moaned the leprechaun.
"I can't decide between new farm tools or a tractor or a fine velvet coat," the farmer replied.
"No, I don't want those!" cried his wife. "I want a new house or some good new boots or a silk dress!"
They glared at each other, unable to agree.

"I'll tell you what. I can see how hard this is for you, so I'll take pity on you," said the leprechaun. "See that rainbow outside? I have hidden a pot of gold at the end of it. It's yours if you go and find it. Then you can buy everything you both want."

The farmer and his wife eagerly agreed. They let the leprechaun go and they set off toward the end of the rainbow. But they never did find that treasure, because you can never outsmart a leprechaun... and you can never get to the end of a rainbow. It moves when you move! That legendary pot of gold will only ever be a sparkling dream.

HOW TO CATCH FOG
Bumps, nets, and webs

Fog is really low-lying cloud. Some plants and animals have found clever ways to collect water from it.

How fog is made

Fog appears when air that is full of water vapor cools close to the ground. This makes the water vapor turn into tiny floating droplets. The bigger and closer together the droplets, the thicker the fog.

GREETINGS FROM FOGGY NEWFOUNDLAND!

The world's foggiest place is Grand Banks, off the coast of Newfoundland in eastern Canada. It has around 200 days of fog every year.

A FOG–DRINKING BEETLE

water-gathering bumps

The little Namib beetle lives in one of the world's driest deserts on the southwestern coast of Africa, where there is no rain to drink. Instead, the beetle uses tiny bumps on its forewings to collect water droplets from fog that rolls in off the sea. The drops then run into the beetle's mouth.

FOG–DRINKING CACTUSES

Cactus plants grow happily in dry deserts because they can get water from the air. Water droplets collect on the cactus spines and bumps, and then get absorbed by the plant. Scientists have even copied cactuses. They have invented materials with bumps and lumps to collect drinking water for humans.

A TREE THAT GATHERS FOG

The dragon's blood tree grows on the island of Socotra in the Indian Ocean. It's shaped like an umbrella, and it gathers fog droplets on its waxy leaves. The droplets roll down the trunk to the tree's roots.

FOG-COLLECTING FOR HUMANS

Communities in the Atacama Desert in Chile collect fog to use as drinking water. The droplets gather on fine mesh nets hung between poles and set up on foggy hillsides. The water drips down into guttering, ready to be collected.

SPIDERS KNOW HOW!

You might notice drops of water on a spider web in foggy weather. The drops gather on the spider silk, at the joints of the web. They make a handy drink for the spider! The silk's sticky coating prevents the web from getting soggy.

SMOG = DIRTY FOG

If fog mixes with lots of pollution—such as soot from factories and fumes from car engines—it turns into smelly, yellowish smog. It's dangerous for people to breathe in smog. In busy polluted cities, smog alerts are sometimes given out to warn everyone to wear breathing masks or stay indoors.

CASPER'S FLOATING FACT

Mist is the same as fog but with more spaced-out droplets, so you can see farther through it.

VISIT A CLOUD FOREST
Where the trees drip fog

Cloud forests are rainforests that are bathed in fog most days, due to their position near the ocean or on a mountainside. Some grow in warm places and some are in colder locations, but they're all full of special animals and plants. I'm going to take you to visit a tropical cloud forest in Guatemala, Central America. It's called the Biotopo del Quetzal reserve.

Epiphytes are plants that grow on other plants without needing to have their roots in soil. They're draped on lots of the trees here. Their roots dangle in the air and soak up water.

Bromeliads are types of epiphyte plants that can gather water in their long, sword-shaped leaves, and store it, too. The biggest in the world can hold gallons of water!

The fog helps lots of plants to grow here, so the forest is very lush. Fog drips from the trees to the ground below, where **ferns**, rare **orchids**, and **mosses** grow.

Geoffroy's spider monkeys swing from tree to tree. When they need a drink, they scoop up water that has gathered in leaf pools.

CASPER'S FLOATING FACT

There are currently thought to be more than 700 cloud forests around the world.

Tree frogs live up in the branches, drinking the water that gathers in tiny pools along the leaves. Can you see a black-eyed tree frog?

Because of all the water and warm weather, there are lots of flowers and fruit, so it's a great place for **insects** such as butterflies and orchid bees to live.

The forest gets its name from the amazing **resplendent quetzal bird**, the national bird of Guatemala. Male resplendent quetzals have shiny green feathers, red tummies, and famously beautiful tail feathers measuring up to 3 feet (90 cm) long.

Reptiles love it here, too. Can you spot a green rax bolay snake curled up on a branch? It might be taking a rest, full of frogs it has eaten!

THE KING OF THE CLOUD FOREST

A weather tale from Central America

How the quetzal got his tail

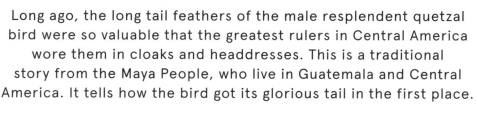

Long ago, the long tail feathers of the male resplendent quetzal bird were so valuable that the greatest rulers in Central America wore them in cloaks and headdresses. This is a traditional story from the Maya People, who live in Guatemala and Central America. It tells how the bird got its glorious tail in the first place.

Many years ago, the Lord of the Maya was a god called Halach-Uinic (hal-ach-you-ee-nic). He liked to rest in the misty cloud forest, but his sleep was often disturbed by the birds screeching, twittering, and hooting at each other.

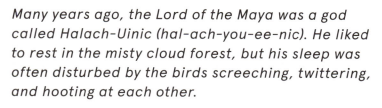

"One of you must be king of the birds and keep the others under control," he declared. *"Who's it going to be?"*

"How about me? I'm such a bright red color, I'd make a splendid-looking king," said the cardinal bird, puffing up his scarlet feathers.

"Wait a minute. Listen to my amazing song. Then you'll choose me, no doubt, because I'm so impressive," the mockingbird interrupted, and broke into a beautiful melody.

"I'm the strongest bird here. I should be leader if you want someone to keep everybody in line," called the turkey, and to show how strong he was, he pushed over a stone.

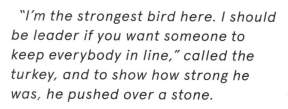

As this was going on, the quetzal bird sat in the shadows, trying to think of something special that would land him the job of king. At that time, he looked rather shabby and uninteresting.
"I haven't got anything to impress, but I know someone who has!" he thought. He flew off to find his friend the roadrunner, who had beautiful long tail feathers.

"Being king is a really busy job, and it's a lot of fuss and bother. You wouldn't want it, Roadrunner. However, I'm prepared to step up and do it for the good of everyone," the quetzal told his friend. "Let me borrow your tail feathers to impress Halach-Uinic. Once he makes me king, I'll bring them back to you and I'll give you riches, too."

The roadrunner didn't want the job of king and he trusted his friend, so he lent the quetzal his wonderful tail feathers. When Halach-Uinic saw them, he was delighted.
"You look incredible, Quetzal! I'll make you king if you lend me those feathers for my headdress every once in a while. Then everyone will see me, even in the fog."

The quetzal became ruler of all the birds in the cloud forest. The only trouble was that he got so busy he forgot about his old friend the roadrunner. You can still hear its call echoing sadly through the cloudy forest.

"PUHUY! PUHUY!"

It means "Where is he? Where is he?" in the language of the Maya.

SNOW DAYS
Snowballs and snowmen

When the weather is really cold, it could soon be time to play in the snow!

When the temperature falls, the water vapor in clouds freezes into tiny ice crystals instead of forming raindrops. The ice crystals may join together to make snowflakes that are heavy enough to fall from the sky.

Snowflakes contain as many as 100 ice crystals, all joined together in a complicated shape.

Most snowflakes have six sides, but every snowflake is slightly different!

Snow can fall at any time of the year toward the North and South Poles. In tropical lands, around the middle of Earth, snow only falls on very high mountaintops, like Mount Kilimanjaro, near the equator, in Africa. In the lands between these areas of the world, snow tends to fall in winter.

COMMON SNOWFLAKE SHAPES

Star

Dendrite

Needle

Plate

Irregular

Snow might be powdery or clumpy, depending on how dry or damp the air is as the snowflakes fall. Clumpy, damp flakes are best for making snowmen and snowballs.

Snowflakes are mostly see-through, like a diamond. They only look white because of the way light reflects off them.

The biggest recorded snowball was almost 33 feet (10 m) wide. That's a greater distance than two midsize cars parked one behind the other.

CASPER'S FLOATING FACT
Japan and Canada are the countries that get the most snow.

BRRR! ICE!
Crackly crystals and icy drips

In winter, you might see frosty fingers on the windows and icicles hanging down from the roof.

ALL ABOUT FROST

For ground frost to form, the night needs to be cold and the ground, too.

Water vapor in the air just above the ground turns into ice crystals and settles on the grass.

CRUNCH!

For frost to form on the outside of a window, the glass needs to be cold. This causes the water vapor in the air around it to turn into ice crystals.

In Northern Europe, there's a legend that Jack Frost brings the frosts in winter. He has spiky frost fingers and hair.

The crystals settle on the glass in patterns that might look like fingers, swirls, or fern leaves.

ALL ABOUT ICICLES

For icicles to form, the winter air temperature needs to keep warming up and cooling down.

When the air warms up a little bit, snow on roofs and tree branches melts and starts to drip down. The drips freeze when the air turns cold again.

DRIP, DRIP!

Icicles get longer and longer as they drip and freeze, then drip and freeze.

Record-breaking icicles can reach 26 feet (8 m) or more!

An ice storm happens when very cold rain falls and instantly freezes over everything. It can coat tree branches and telephone lines in thick ice.

CASPER'S FLOATING FACT

Frost forms at night because that's when it's coldest.

29

SOPHIE AND THE BARBEGAZI

A weather tale from Switzerland

Big feet and new friends

This story is inspired by the legend of the Barbegazi, gnomes who are said to live high in the snowy mountains of the Alps in Switzerland.

High up in the Alps, in a cozy hidden cave, there lived a Barbegazi called Frostbeard. His hair and beard looked like white icicles, and—like all Barbegazi—he had extra-big feet, which came in handy as skis in the snow. Meanwhile, down in the valley below his mountain, there lived a farmer's daughter called Sophie. In springtime every year, her sheep trotted partway up the mountain to graze on the sweet grass below the snowline.

Frostbeard had heard humans skiing past his cave, making lots of noise and messing up the snow. He thought they sounded rather frightening, so he stayed away from them. Meanwhile, Sophie had never met a Barbegazi and she thought they sounded a bit scary.

One day, Sophie was about to set off up the path to check on the sheep. At the same time, high above the snowline, Frostbeard came out of his cave when...

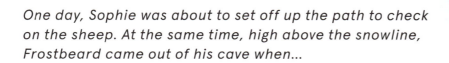

RUMBLE!

TUMBLE!

Snow began to tumble down the mountain in a great wave. It was an avalanche! Frostbeard was able to surf smoothly down on top of it, using his big feet as skis. As Sophie watched from below, he began rescuing the sheep one by one from under the snow, using his feet as shovels! Then he rushed back up to his cave, thinking nobody had seen him.

The next time Frostbeard ventured out, he found a surprise. A delicious cheese had been placed outside his door, along with a jug of cream and a newly knitted woolly hat. Puzzled, he crept down the mountainside—following a line of footprints in the snow—until he found Sophie.

"Er... hello. You're a Barbegazi, aren't you?" she said, nervously.

"Er... hello. You're a human, aren't you?" he replied, feeling just as nervous.

They chatted and Sophie discovered that Frostbeard was not scary, just shy. Frostbeard discovered that humans can be thoughtful, after all. They had both made a new friend. All it took was some kindness and two "hellos" in the snow!

WHICH WAY, WIND?

Look out for the zooming molecules!

You might sometimes see clouds moving in the sky. They're being pushed along by the wind.

Wind is caused by invisible **air molecules** moving in the sky. They zoom around fast if they are warm, but float slowly if they are cold. They rise when they warm up and sink when they cool down.

We can't see air molecules moving this way and that, but we can feel them as wind. They might move gently along as a breeze or tear along at top speed, making strong gusts. The strongest winds can move faster than a high-speed train.

Wind can even change the shape of rocks. If it blows against soft rock for many years, particles (such as specks of sand) carried along by the wind can slowly grind the rock down. This is known as **erosion**.

Wind can make you feel much colder by blowing away heat from your skin. It's an effect called **windchill**, and it's the reason why you should wrap up extra-warm on a windy day.

Stone statues can be worn down by the wind and weather. The famous sphinx statue in Egypt has been worn down by sandstorms whipped up by wind.

OOOH! HERE I GO!

You might hear strong wind **whistling** or even howling. It's not the wind itself making the noise. Instead, the sound is created when the air hits an object such as a tree, a building, or ocean waves.

NAMING THE WIND

Regular winds are given their own names.
Here are a few of them:

Berg in South Africa, **Chinook** in the Rocky Mountains of the USA and Canada, **Bora** in Italy, Croatia, and Slovenia

Etesian in Greece, **Harmattan** in West Africa, **Khamsin** in Egypt

Some winds blow regularly across an area of land or sea. They are called **prevailing winds**. Sometimes you can spot which direction a prevailing wind blows because trees may grow leaning the same way.

CASPER'S FLOATING FACT
On the planet Neptune, wind blows as fast as the fastest jet plane!

WATCH OUT: STORMS ABOUT!
Cracking, rumbling sky sounds

When my friend the cumulonimbus cloud turns up,
there might soon be noisy flashes and rumbles.

A **cumulonimbus cloud** forms when warm air that's full of water vapor rushes upward, higher and higher. Inside the cloud, strong winds buffet everything around. A charge of electricity gradually builds up.

You can spot a cumulonimbus cloud because it towers up into the sky and the top spreads out wide and flat. The cloud might be dark gray at the bottom.

Eventually... **CRACK!** The electricity flows down to Earth from the clouds, then zips back up as a superfast **bolt of lightning**.

The path around the lightning gets incredibly hot, up to five times as hot as the Sun.

You might sometimes see **forked lightning**, which zigzags up, or **sheet lightning**, which flashes between clouds.

CRACK!

Lightning can be deadly and can cause fires where it strikes. It tends to hit a tall point when it reaches Earth, such as a tree or a tall building.

BOOM!

Thunder is the sound of air spreading out very quickly when it heats up in the path of lightning.

Thunder happens at the same time as lightning, but we see the light before we hear the sound. The louder the sound you hear, the closer the lightning is to you.

Count the seconds between seeing lightning and hearing thunder to figure out roughly how far away a storm is. It's about 0.6 miles (1 km) away for every three seconds.

The biggest thunderclouds can stretch up to 16 miles (25 km) wide and many thousands of feet up, higher than passenger planes fly.

CASPER'S FLOATING FACT

There are around 40,000 thunderstorms on Earth every day.

WHIRLING WEATHER
Spinning clouds and roaring winds

Hold on to your hat! It's time to meet **hurricanes** and **tornadoes**, the world's strongest whirling clouds.

Hurricanes form over the oceans around the equator—the middle section of Earth. They build up when warm air that's full of water vapor rises upward over a really large area. Storm clouds form high above and strong winds begin to whirl around and around.

Satellites can take pictures of hurricanes from space. A hurricane image will show a hole, called an eye, in the center of the whirling clouds. The eye is a patch of calm weather in the middle of all the roaring winds.

This is what a hurricane looks like from above.

Other names for a hurricane are typhoon and cyclone.

The wind speed in the strongest hurricanes is 155 mph (250 kp/h) an hour or more.

A hurricane can last for two or three days.

If a hurricane reaches land it can cause lots of damage. Out at sea, giant hurricane waves have been known to reach 98 feet (30 m) high—roughly as tall as a 10-story building!

The US Air Force Hurricane Hunter Squad flies planes into hurricanes off the US coast. They gather information to predict how strong a storm will get and which way it will go.

There's another kind of whirling wind—a tornado, or twister. It's a funnel of spinning air that forms underneath storm clouds, then zooms across the ground.

A moving tornado damages everything in its path and sucks up anything loose, just like a vacuum cleaner. An area in the midwestern USA, nicknamed Tornado Alley, gets the most tornadoes in the world—roughly 120 a year.

If a tornado forms over an ocean or a lake, it can suck up water to make a spinning **waterspout**. It might even suck up fish, then drop them back down in a fishy shower!

CASPER'S FLOATING FACT
The most powerful tornado wind ever measured reached over 298 mph (480 kp/h) an hour.

TIGER, TIGER, THE WIND IS COMING!

An African American weather tale

A breezy lesson

This story is inspired by a traditional African American folk tale.

Once long ago, in a jungle far, far away, there was a year when the rains were late coming. It got very hard for the animals to find food or water. Soon there was only one tree left. It was beautiful and laden with juicy fruit, but it was guarded by a greedy tiger!

The other animals decided to send Rabbit to persuade Tiger to share the fruit. As Rabbit crept towards the tree...

Grrrrr!

Tiger roared fiercely.
  "Come on, Tiger. You should share food in this time of trouble. It's only fair," said Rabbit.

Tiger just roared louder.
  "Grrrrr! I'll eat YOU if you come any closer," he threatened.

Rabbit retreated to where the other animals were gathered.

"Any luck?" asked Elephant.

"Sorry. Tiger won't share anything," sighed Rabbit.

"We're all starving! We have to do something," cried Monkey.

"Hmm. I think I have a plan," Rabbit replied, and he began to explain...

Later that day, Tiger was sitting under his tree when Rabbit turned up again, carrying a long coil of rope.

"Oh dear! Oh my! A great wind is coming and it's going to blow us all off the planet!" he muttered, loud enough for Tiger to hear.

"What did you say?" called Tiger.

"I said that a great wind is coming and it's going to blow us all off the planet!" cried Rabbit. "I must go. I've promised to tie my animal friends down so they won't be blown away."

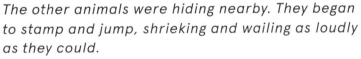

The other animals were hiding nearby. They began to stamp and jump, shrieking and wailing as loudly as they could.

"Oh no! The wind has arrived!" cried Rabbit.

"Tie me down! Quickly!" shouted Tiger over the din.

"Are you sure?" asked Rabbit.

"Yes, yes! Do it!" cried Tiger, as the other animals increased their noise and made the ground tremble with their stamping.

Rabbit tied Tiger tightly to the tree so that he couldn't escape. Then the other animals came out and helped themselves to the fruit.

"The great wind brought you a great lesson, eh, Tiger? In times of need, you shouldn't be selfish. Ha ha! I'll bet that lesson really blew you away," laughed Rabbit. He was right, of course, and even Tiger had to admit that the great wind had made him look a great fool that day!

SUNSHINE DAYS
Sunsets and sun tricks

Our super-powerful Sun is the ruler of the weather. It sends the heat that makes air molecules whiz around and clouds form.

Sunlight sometimes puts on a show at **sunrise** or **sunset**, when the clouds turn orange and pink. This is caused by the sunlight scattering as it passes through the air. The red and orange parts of the light scatter the least, so they're easiest to see.

You can sometimes see for yourself when the warm Sun has heated up the ground. Light bends as it travels through the warm air rising above the ground, making the landscape look wobbly. This is known as a **heat haze**.

Sunlight can play tricks on us. In a desert you might see a patch of water on the horizon that doesn't really exist. It's called a **mirage** and it's really the sky reflected onto hot air just above the ground. If you were a thirsty desert explorer, you would be disappointed!

A special type of mirage called a **Fata Morgana** has sometimes puzzled sailors. It makes ships and islands look as if they are floating in the air above the sea on the horizon.

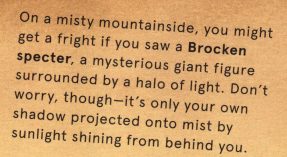

On a misty mountainside, you might get a fright if you saw a **Brocken specter**, a mysterious giant figure surrounded by a halo of light. Don't worry, though—it's only your own shadow projected onto mist by sunlight shining from behind you.

The sunniest place on Earth is the desert city of Yuma in Arizona, USA. It has 4,015 hours of sunshine each year, which is over 300 sunny days.

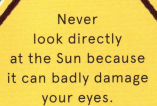

Never look directly at the Sun because it can badly damage your eyes.

CASPER'S FLOATING FACT

It takes sunlight 8 minutes and 20 seconds to reach Earth from the Sun, 93 million miles (150 million km) away.

LIVING IN A HOT HOME

Staying out of the sunshine

Clouds can keep us cool, but how do animals survive when the sunshine is superhot and clouds are nowhere to be seen?

One of the hottest places on Earth is Death Valley in California, USA. Summer temperatures here are so warm that visitors say it feels like walking into an oven. It's also one of the driest places, with just 2 inches (5 cm) of rain all year.

Bighorn sheep roam the mountain slopes. They can go without water for several days. If they do find water, they can drink several gallons at a time.

Jackrabbits have oversized ears that act like radiators. Their body heat gets released through the ears, helping to keep them cool.

Most Death Valley animals only come out when it's cool—at dusk, dawn, or through the night. The rest of the time, they hide in the shade of rocks or in burrows.

Coyotes hunt in the cool of the evening or even in the dark of night. They communicate with each other in the gloom by yipping or barking.

Kangaroo rats don't have to drink. They get all the water they need from the plants they eat. They don't even need water to wash. Instead, they roll around in the sand to take a dust bath.

Sidewinder snakes slither sideways so that their bodies hardly ever touch the hot ground. When it's really hot they hide in burrows or lie buried just underneath the sand.

Desert tortoises stay mostly in burrows underground, where they rest up and wait for cool weather. They only come out for around 100 days of the year.

CASPER'S FLOATING FACT
Hot sun is dangerous to humans, too! Always wear sunscreen and a hat in warm sunshine.

THE CLOUD—SCRAPING LADY

A weather tale from Canada

Why the weather changes

Once, two brothers were walking back along the shore to their village. Before they could reach home, the sky filled with thick dark clouds, blocking out the Sun. The wind blew up, and soon there was a fearsome blizzard that almost knocked the boys off their feet into a pile of snow!

They ran to the nearest shelter—a small house perched on its own with a view over the ocean. When they knocked on the door, a kindly old lady invited them in.

"My goodness! You shouldn't be out in this weather. Come inside to get warm and dry," she said. She sat them by the fire and gave them each a bowl of steaming soup.

Then she put on her coat and her soft reindeer-skin boots, and slipped a sharp stone tool into her pocket.

"It's time I went out to do something very important, but you must stay here. WHATEVER YOU DO, don't come outside to see!" she warned as she left.
"What's she up to?" one of the brothers asked once she had gone.

"I don't know. That was a stone scraper she picked up, liked the one Dad uses when he makes reindeer furs into rugs and coats," his brother replied. "Let's go and see what she's doing. It'll be OK. We'll stay out of sight and she won't know we're watching." They tiptoed to the door, pushed it open a little way, and crept outside.

What they saw amazed them. The old lady was high up in the air above their heads, sitting on a storm cloud! She was scraping away at it with her stone tool, and where she had scraped through, there were patches of blue sky and rays of sunshine. The more she worked, the sunnier it got.

"Wow! That's clever!" cried the brothers, too loudly.

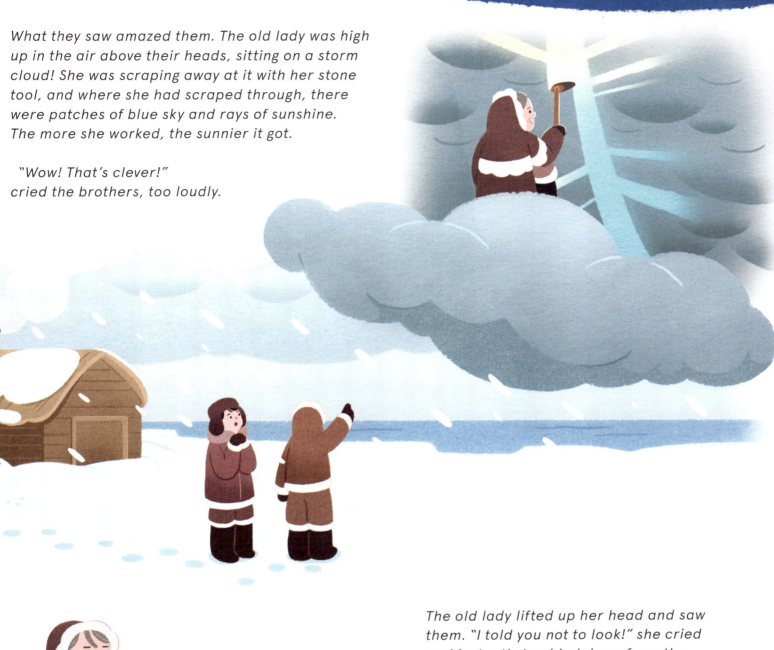

The old lady lifted up her head and saw them. "I told you not to look!" she cried and instantly tumbled down from the cloud. Luckily she landed in a soft pile of snow, but she was very angry.

"I could have scraped all the storm clouds away for good, but I won't be able to finish the job now because you broke the magic spell," she grumbled. "I can't ever go up again, so that's that. I only cleaned away half of the clouds, so we're going to have mixed weather from now on—sometimes stormy and sometimes sunny. That's how it's going to be around here forever and ever." And she was right!

BE A WATER AND CLOUD FRIEND

Clouds are made of Earth's water, going around and around in the water cycle. You can help keep the water clean and safe by doing small but important things, and getting your friends and family to do the same.

BE CAREFUL WHAT YOU ADD

It's best to use water-friendly soaps and cleansers. They will do less harm when they wash into the water. Get your family to look for products marked "eco-friendly."

HELP KEEP THE WATER CLEAN

Make sure you never leave litter on the ground, especially plastic waste. It washes into streams and oceans, polluting the water. Litter can do harm to creatures, too—they might swallow it or get tangled in it. So always dispose of it safely.

TRY NOT TO WASTE WATER

Sometimes, when the weather is hot, water can be in short supply. It's called a drought (drout). Do your best not to waste water so there's always enough to go around.

HELP THE WORLD TO GET WATER

Around one in five children in the world can't easily get clean water to drink. Many organizations try to help by campaigning for clean water and by digging water wells. Next time your school holds an event to raise money for charity, you could suggest sending some to a water charity.

It can be annoying when it rains
and you can't go outside to play,
but really Earth is a lucky place
to have the water it needs for life.
Enjoy the sound of the pattering drops,
and splash in puddles when it stops!

Be sure to use your crayons and paints
to make sky pictures of what you see,
with lovely colors and clouds like me.

With love from,

Casper the cloud x

For Vivian, who made all these and is a star. - M.B.

To Moira, who embodies all the magic and wonder that made this possible. - V.M.